ABOUT THE AUTHOR

Jonathan Litton studied science, philosophy and education at Cambridge University and has written and edited numerous children's non-fiction books on topics ranging from cities to space, maths to languages, and physics to philosophy. He lives in northern Japan with his wife Kaori, son Eiji and daughter Isla, where he combines teaching, writing and exploring the great outdoors.

ABOUT THE ARTIST

Wenjia Tang is a freelance illustrator who graduated from Maryland Institute College of Art in 2017. She was born in southeast China and came to the US for high school when she was 15. She loves all kinds of animals, and lives with a cat in Manhattan, New York. Her work has been recognised by American Illustration, Society of Illustrators, AOI and 3x3 Magazine among others.

The Forest Stewardship Council ® (FSC®) is an international, non-governmental organisation dedicated to promoting responsible management of the world's forests. FSC operates a system of forest certification and product labelling that allows consumers to identify wood and wood-based products from well-managed forests and other controlled sources.

For more information about the FSC, please visit their website at www.fsc.org

LITTLE TIGER
LONDON

360 DEGREES
An imprint of the Little Tiger Group
1 Coda Studios, 189 Munster Road, London SW6 6AW
Imported into the EEA by Penguin Random House Ireland,
Morrison Chambers, 32 Nassau Street, Dublin D02 YH68
www.littletiger.co.uk
First published in Great Britain 2021
Text copyright © 2021 Jonathan Litton
Illustrations copyright © 2021 Wenjia Tang
A CIP catalogue record for this book is
available from the British Library
All rights reserved
Printed in China
ISBN: 978-1-84857-942-2
CPB/2700/1749/0321
10 9 8 7 6 5 4 3 2 1

INTRODUCTION

Humans are thirsty for knowledge. The clue is in the name – scientists call our species Homo sapiens, meaning 'wise person'. How do we become wise? Through discoveries! From Antarctica to Everest and from ocean trenches to the depths of space, human minds are keen to unravel the mysteries of the universe.

Often the discoveries come from questions – what's over the horizon? What happens if you fly a kite in a thunderstorm? Why do apples drop from trees?

LET'S FIND OUT!

CONTENTS

7. INTRO TO HISTORY
- 8. DRAGON BONES AND DINOSAURS
- 10. PREHISTORIC PARADE
- 12. HUMAN DISCOVERY
- 14. LOST WORLDS
- 16. ANCIENT ARTEFACTS
- 18. REWRITTEN HISTORY

19. INTRO TO EARTH
- 20. ENDS OF THE EARTH
- 22. OCEANS
- 24. EARTH: INSIDE AND OUT
- 26. NEW SPECIES… AND OLD ONES
- 28. HIDDEN GEMS

29. INTRO TO SCIENCE
- 30. EUREKA MOMENTS
- 32. ACCIDENTAL DISCOVERIES
- 34. EXPERIMENTAL DISCOVERIES

The world is an ever-changing place: discoveries are made, records are broken, new facts are found, and history recovered. We will be happy to revise and update information in future editions.

36. ELEMENTS
38. ATOMS
40. BODIES AND BRAINS
42. ALL CREATURES GREAT AND SMALL
44. MATHS
46. BOTANICAL BREAKTHROUGHS

47. INTRO TO SPACE

48. AS OLD AS THE STARS
50. THE SOLAR SYSTEM
52. DEEP SPACE
54. DARK SPACE
56. STRANGE SPACE
58. UNDISCOVERED SPACE

59. NATURE OF DISCOVERIES

60. AGAINST THE ODDS
62. ANATOMY OF DISCOVERIES
64. WHATEVER NEXT?

"GIVE ME A PLACE TO STAND AND A LEVER LONG ENOUGH, AND I WILL MOVE THE WORLD."

ARCHIMEDES

INTRODUCTION TO HISTORY

Some discoveries shine new light on well-known parts of history, and others open up understanding of millions of years of events we didn't even know occurred. The fossilised remains of prehistoric life were sensational finds, and as we continue to unearth evidence of ancient beasts, we gain a clearer picture of the world before us.

We learn lots about ancient civilisations from archaeological remains, and every now and then we stumble across remarkable windows into former worlds.

DRAGON BONES AND DINOSAURS

Dinosaurs may be old news to us, but imagine discovering fossils and footprints of huge creatures before the word 'dinosaur' existed, before the Jurassic Park movies, and before the concepts of evolution, extinction, and geological time (stretching back billions of years, not just thousands). Such findings must have been fantastical beyond all belief.

Even today, we know very little about dinosaurs. Only a fraction gets preserved, so many will have disappeared without trace.

TERRIBLE LIZARDS

Dinosaur discoveries came thick and fast in the early 1800s...

1809, William Smith found an Iguanodon bone.
1822, Gideon Mantell found an Iguanodon tooth and saw that this ancient beast was huge.
1832, Mantell discovered Hylaeosaurus.
1841, Richard Owen suggested the word dinosaur or 'terrible lizard'.

SUE (90% COMPLETE T-REX REMAINS)

A T-REX NAMED SUE

67 million years ago, a 28-year-old T-Rex died. Its body was covered with mud in conditions perfect for the formation of fossils. In 1990, American Sue Hendrickson found some T-Rex bones in South Dakota and called on the rest of the team to look for more. Sue had discovered the most complete T-Rex fossils ever found, and the dinosaur specimen has been unofficially named after her.

EARLY INTERPRETATIONS

The Chinese have several records of 'dragon bones' and, in the 6th century BCE, Xenophanes of Greece wrote of fish fossils found in quarries near Syracuse. He took them as evidence that the whole substance of the world – earth, sea, and rock – had once been mingled. In the 1st century CE, Pliny the Elder realised that amber came from fossilised pine trees and in 1027, the Persian naturalist Avicenna correctly explained the stoniness of fossils. People from all cultures have made discoveries about our planet's prehistoric past.

BONE WARS

American palaeontologists Othniel Charles Marsh and Edward Drinker Cope were great rivals, and from 1877 to 1892, they rushed to discover as many dinosaurs as possible. They also sabotaged each other's efforts – with theft, fire, blackmail, and even poison! They discovered 142 new species of dinosaurs... or did they? Today, only 32 of those discoveries are valid, as many of the new 'species' were in fact duplicates.

OTHNIEL CHARLES MARSH

EDWARD DRINKER COPE

You can visit Sue at the Field Museum of Natural History in Chicago, USA.

RECENT DISCOVERIES

Dinosaurs are being discovered at a faster rate than ever before – a new species per week on average! Why? Because more palaeontologists have been trained, technology has improved, and countries with promising rock formations have opened up to scientific examination.

Few discoveries are as impressive as the 15m- (49ft-) long Ledumahadi mafube dinosaur remains discovered in South Africa – its name means **GIANT THUNDERCLAP AT DAWN!**

GIANT THUNDERCLAP

SHE SELLS SEA SHELLS

MARY ANNING

Born into poverty in 1799, Mary Anning used to walk by the sea with her dog, Tray. She learned how to find little fossils from her father who sold them to tourists but, after he died, she found she had a knack for finding bigger ones! She and her brother, Joseph, found an ichthyosaur skeleton in 1811 and 1812, which put her on the map as one of the greatest fossil-finders ever known.

PREHISTORIC PARADE

Dinosaurs are the superstars of prehistoric life (with pterosaurs and plesiosaurs as the supporting acts), but they only roamed the Earth for about 4% of its history. The remaining 96% of prehistoric life included some weird and wonderful species, and our discoveries cover just a fraction of these...

WOOLLY MAMMOTH

Scientists have recently made a number of discoveries about the woolly mammoth. Firstly, they found a specimen so fresh it still had blood inside. Secondly, they found a month-old calf which still had milk in its belly. And thirdly, they found evidence that an isolated population lived on Wrangel Island in the Arctic Ocean until about 4,000 years ago – much more recent than previous estimates.

NURALAGUS REX

A giant prehistoric rabbit, discovered by a teenager in Spain.

GLYPTODON

This armoured mammal was discovered in the 18th century.

MEGATHERIUM

This giant ground sloth, discovered in Argentina in 1788, measured up to 1.8m (6ft) from snout to tail.

BUNOSTEGOS
Discovered in 2003, this gentle giant is the earliest creature known to have walked on four legs.

AEGIROCASSIS
This weird sea creature' belongs to a group called 'anomalocaridids', meaning 'abnormal shrimp.'

CAMEROCERAS
When finding super-long cones, some early discoverers thought they had found unicorn horns!

DICKINSONIA
Recent research declared this strange beast to be the earliest known animal big enough to see without a microscope.

MICROFOSSILS
Some of the oldest rocks in the world can be found in Australia. In 1982, a chunk of rock was collected by J William Schopf and his team. This rock contained tiny fossils of early life… or did it? In 1993, other scientists challenged the claim, and Schopf published further evidence in 2002 and 2017, which the scientific community finally accepted.

HUMAN DISCOVERY

Archaeologists (people who study the past through physical evidence) and anthropologists (people who study humans) have been able to mark humankind's march across the globe using clues such as bones, tools, pottery, evidence of agriculture, and fire control. The earliest sign of humans is in Africa.

Gradually, humans discovered other parts of Africa and the Middle East. They developed agriculture – which changed human history – and ventured deeper into Asia and Europe. The Americas were reached by land and sea, and Australia and Oceania were reached by ocean voyages.

6 Iceland was the earliest discovery in written history as the Viking Sagas give detailed accounts of the island's discovery in 874 CE.

LUCY

1 Lucy, also known as Dinkinesh, is human's earliest known ancestor, dating from 3.2 million years ago. She was found in Ethiopia in 1974.

2 The earliest evidence of agriculture comes from about 10,000 years ago in the Fertile Crescent, located in what we now call the Middle East.

What might change on this map with new discoveries? Will Lucy's great-great-great ancestor be uncovered? Will some dates change and some arrows point in different directions? Our knowledge of our ancestors' discoveries is still very much a work in progress!

3 Humans are thought to have crossed a land bridge from Asia to the Americas 20,000 years ago.

4 Indonesian sailors arrived in Madagascar about 1,200 years ago after a journey of around 7,500km (4,660mi). One writer has called this "the single most astonishing fact of human geography for the entire world."

5 With no humans until about 1300CE, New Zealand was the last major landmass to be discovered... except Antarctica.

LOST WORLDS

It seems extraordinary that whole cities can become lost, but around the world today there are many 'ghost towns', from Pripyat in Ukraine (abandoned due to the Chernobyl nuclear disaster in 1986) to St Kilda in Scotland (where all the villagers left the island for an easier life), to name just two examples. This can and does happen to whole cities.

POMPEII

In 79CE, the sudden eruption of Mount Vesuvius buried the Roman city of Pompeii in lava and ash. People were clearly unprepared for the disaster as their bodies were found doing everyday tasks at the time of destruction.

MACHU PICCHU
PERU

Machu Picchu, in the Peruvian Andes, was built by the Incas 500 years ago. American explorer Hiram Bingham is often credited with 'rediscovering' it in 1911, but he was guided there by a local, Melchor Arteaga, and some of the stones already had graffiti on them, so it wasn't exactly 'lost' after all!

GREAT ZIMBABWE

The walled city of Great Zimbabwe contained important people and resources, and its influence stretched across southern Africa, before it fell into decline and became 'lost' to the larger world.

Many Europeans have claimed discovery of the great city... and some didn't believe that ancient Africans could have built such a fine place. They were wrong. Now, at long last, it is protected.

VINLAND

In around 1000CE, Leif Erikson sailed from Europe to North America where he founded Vinland... the Viking homeland on this new continent.

In the 1970s, near the present-day site of St Louis, USA, archaeologists discovered thousand-year-old Cahokia – the largest pre-Columbian city north of Mexico. This trading hub may have been the largest urban centre on the planet in its heyday.

CAHOKIA

ANGKOR
CAMBODIA

MILLIONS of tourists a year come to marvel at the ancient temples, statues, walls, and buildings of this 12th-century city in the Cambodian jungle. In 2007, Damian Evans and Jean-Baptiste Chevance used space-age radar technology to do a full survey of the area and found that the city was as large as modern-day Los Angeles!

The ruins of the ancient city of Pompeii are thought to have been first successfully excavated by Domenico Fontana in the 16th century. Excavations have spanned **HUNDREDS** of years.

About a thousand years later, Norwegians Helge Ingstad and Anne Stine Ingstad finally located the lost city, using archaeological techniques and knowledge of the Viking sagas.

TROY

Ancient Greek stories spoke of a city called Troy, but scholars debated its existence for centuries. German archaeologist Heinrich Schliemann let his spade do the talking – in 1870 he dug at a site in Turkey and unearthed the mysterious city… and its gold, which he quickly smuggled out of the country!

There were actually nine versions of Troy, each built on top of the previous one, following a series of natural disasters.

15

ANCIENT ARTEFACTS

Coins, jewellery, skulls, tools, paintings, and writing – our ancestors left plenty of clues behind for us to learn about their lives. However, many human-made objects have been destroyed over time, making discovery difficult and the ancient artefacts very rare. Here are just a few...

ROSETTA STONE

In 1799, a French soldier near Rosetta in Egypt discovered a huge dark stone with three types of writing on it: Egyptian hieroglyphs, Demotic (a language of ancient Egypt) and ancient Greek. As the writing said the same thing in three languages, it was the key to unlocking the secrets of hieroglyphs.

French scholar Jean-François Champollion is credited with the major breakthroughs that led to the reading of the hieroglyphs. It is said that he ran down the street shouting: "Je tiens mon affaire!" (*I'VE GOT IT!*) but collapsed from his excitement!

TUTANKHAMUN'S TOMB

Egypt is a real treasure trove where many wonders have been unearthed. The Valley of the Kings is a site where ancient pharaohs were buried, and an impressive looking burial chamber was discovered there in 1922.

However, it took time to open it, and Egyptologists were astonished to discover King Tutankhamun's 3,300-year-old mummified body there in 1925, beneath a golden death mask. This is one of the most stunning ancient artefacts found anywhere in the world.

16

DEAD SEA SCROLLS

The land around the Dead Sea is hot and dry. The indigenous Bedouin people herded goats there, throwing stones to keep stray animals on the right path. One day in the late 1940s, a **SMASH** was heard as a stone entered a cave – but what could it have broken in this deserted land?

The answer was a clay jar that contained an ancient scroll dating back about 2,000 years. It wasn't the only one – fragments from 981 different manuscripts have been collected from 11 caves. Their content gives a window into the world two millennia ago.

LASCAUX CAVE PAINTINGS

In 1940, four boys and their dog, Robot, were walking in southwest France. Robot stopped to dig near a fallen tree, and the boys wondered if the dog could be leading them to a legendary tunnel and a lost treasure. Amazingly, when the boys took over the digging duties, they found an entrance to a cave in which they discovered wall-paintings, mainly of animals, thought to be up to 20,000 years old.

TERRACOTTA ARMY

In 1974, local farmers were digging a well near Xi'an in central China. On their fifth day of digging, they unearthed a life-size human figure made of terracotta, a type of clay.

They went on to find bronze arrows, crossbows, and pieces of pottery. Their well was never finished – they called in expert archaeologists who continued the digging and discovered that this ancient, imperial tomb contained more than 8,000 warriors, 600 horses, and 150 chariots, with no two figures identical.

REWRITTEN HISTORY

Some discoveries cause history to be rewritten... Evolution redefined our relationship with animals, and geological and astronomical discoveries showed that the Earth was much older and the universe much bigger than we had previously thought. These discoveries changed our ideas of prehistory.

ABORIGINAL ARTEFACTS

A 2017 discovery in Australia has altered our understanding of the human migration story. Sharpened axes and grindstones were found dating back at least 65,000 years... which means humans arrived in Australia much earlier than previously thought.

This in turn rewrites much of the trek out of Africa and raises the possibility that the ancestors of Aboriginal people could have been among the first cultures to make long sea voyages. The axes were highly advanced – no specimens with polished and sharpened edges would be found from other cultures for a further 20,000 years.

FIRE CONTROL

When our ancestors discovered how to make and control fire, it was life-changing. But when did this discovery take place?

The traditional view was that fire control was probably cultivated in the last 500,000 years, with a site in Israel offering one of the earliest known examples. But new evidence, found at Wonderwerk Cave in South Africa, pushes the date back to one million years ago. And some archaeologists believe in even earlier evidence...

18

INTRODUCTION TO EARTH

Our home has a huge amount of undiscovered territory, from the innermost regions to the depths of the oceans. We know more about the Moon than some parts of our own planet.

But, we have made some startling discoveries, from amazing 'new' species to 'old' ones thought to have been extinct for thousands of years; from the tropical rainforests to the icy polar regions; and from the mountaintops to the core of the Earth itself.

ENDS OF THE EARTH

The ends of the Earth are magnets for the adventurous. Difficult to reach, difficult to explore, and unlike anywhere else on Earth, the poles have invited the *BEST* and the *BRAVEST* to uncover their secrets, from passages through the wilderness to volcanoes, lakes, and the incredible wildlife of the regions.

ANTARCTICA: LAST LAND?

In 1819, the Spanish ship San Telmo became shipwrecked in the southern seas. Remains of some of the crew were later found on Livingston Island, just off the Antarctic mainland. Could they have been the continent's first explorers?

In 1820, Russian explorers Fabian Gottlieb von Bellingshausen and Mikhail Lazarev saw the ice shelf of Antarctica and brought their findings back home so have been 'officially' credited with the discovery.

Two further sightings were made in 1820, and then in 1821, an American expedition led by Captain John Davis set foot on the Antarctic Peninsula. "I think this Southern Land to be a Continent," he wrote. Finally, humans had arrived on Antarctica.

NORTHWEST AND NORTHEAST PASSAGES

For centuries, Europeans dreamed of a shortcut to Asia through Arctic waters. Robert McClure and John Rae both came close to navigating a route, and Roald Amundsen of Norway completed the discovery of the Northwest Passage in 1906.

Honours for the discovery of the slightly less famous Northeast Passage (above Siberia) go to Swedish-Finnish explorer Adolf Erik Nordenskiöld who completed the trip in 1878.

ROBERT McCLURE   JOHN RAE

ROALD AMUNDSEN   ADOLF ERIK NORDENSKIÖLD

NORTHERNMOST LAND

The North Pole's ice floats on the Arctic Ocean; no land lies beneath it. However, in 2007, Dennis Schmitt spotted the island of Stray Dog West amidst the white ice of northern waters. This may be the northernmost land on Earth. One previous record-holding island seems to have been eroded by ice and, with rising sea levels, Stray Dog West's future is uncertain too.

HIDING UNDER THE ICE

Perhaps the greatest discoveries are hiding under ice. Not only have dinosaur remains and a valley deeper than the Grand Canyon been found, but in 1958, a team of scientists were surprised to find a huge chain of mountains under their feet when checking the depth of ice with dynamite!

There are even huge 'subglacial lakes' (water under the ice), where scientists found not just microbes but also fish. In this environment, disconnected from sunlight, the microbes draw energy and nutrients from methane, and ammonia from sediment hundreds of thousands of years old. This discovery opens up the possibility of the existence of life on other planets.

ANTARCTIC LIFE

About 1-2% of the continent is ice-free, allowing only brave plants to settle. Mosses and lichens cling to rocks and draw water and minerals from their surroundings.

You'll find visitors from the sea (such as penguins and seals), but you'll have to get your microscope out for Antarctic land animals. Growing up to 5mm (0.2in) long, the mighty tardigrade is the king of the continent. Also known as the water bear, this remarkable creature can survive nuclear explosions and even being **BLASTED** into space!

OCEANS

While 'explorers' used to flit across the oceans in search of 'new' land (that was almost always previously discovered), the real treasure lay beneath their boats. The world's oceans still include vast unexplored areas – it's estimated that 95% of the volume has so far escaped our attention. That's a staggering statistic.

When we do take a look, we make thousands of discoveries. Ocean explorers have unearthed many new species, whole new ecosystems, and even a previously unknown zone of ocean life. Let's dive in for a small sample of deep-sea discoveries...

PLANKTON

The oceans are full of plankton, whose name means 'wanderers'. Plant-like phytoplankton collect energy from sunlight using photosynthesis, and animal-like zooplankton get their energy from eating phytoplankton. The first step in the ocean food chain, they produce 50% of the world's oxygen but were only discovered in the 1980s and probably 90% of their species are yet to be known to scientists.

MICROSCOPIC PLANKTON

INTO THE DEEP

Adaptation is key to survival in the ocean depths, where there's little light and massive pressure. Over millennia, shallow-water species have been able to delve deeper and deeper, morphing into specialist survivors in their extreme environment. Only a fraction of these fantastical beasts have yet been discovered...

VENUS FLY TRAP ANEMONE

YETI CRAB

COCKATOO SQUID

GHOST OCTOPUS

MOUNTAINS

It's rare for new mountains to be discovered on land. But in the oceans, thousands of mountains have recently been revealed. Instead of diving down to discover them, the findings have been made from space: satellite imaging has allowed us to see thousands of peaks we had no idea existed.

PLASTIC

A sad discovery was made on Henderson Island, which is located about halfway between New Zealand and Chile: the island is home to more than 38 million pieces of plastic. This is despite no human residents. The island sits at a crossroads of ocean currents and sweeps up rubbish from all corners of the globe.

"WE HAVE TURNED THE OCEAN INTO A PLASTIC SOUP,"

said Enric Sala, the scientist who made this shocking discovery.

SEA SPIDER

LIGHTLESS LIFE

In the deepest, darkest depths, new ecosystems have been discovered around hydrothermal vents where the lowest in the food chain draw their energy from minerals ejected from the vents rather than from sunlight.

Researchers were amazed when they discovered this. What could it mean for finding life in other hostile environments, including on other planets?

NEW OCEAN LAYER: RARIPHOTIC ZONE

In 2018, oceanographers searching underwater mountains off the coast of Bermuda found over 100 new species and discovered a whole new ocean layer: the rariphotic zone.

One of the team commented:

"WE'VE BEEN LOOKING UP WHEN WE SHOULD HAVE BEEN LOOKING DOWN."

Space missions have gained more funding than ocean exploration, despite the oceans holding so many secrets.

SUN STAR

23

EARTH: INSIDE AND OUT

INNER EARTH

We surface-dwellers have often questioned what's beneath our feet. Our glimpses inside the planet have been very limited, but ingenious techniques have rewarded us with some astonishing discoveries, such as an inner inner core and a giant suboceanic 'sponge'.

STRUCTURE OF EARTH

Tracking the path of seismic waves (earthquake waves) through the planet gives us data about the internal structure; primary (P) waves will travel right through the core, but in modified paths. Their shadow zones reveal the structure. Secondary (S) waves are stopped by the core, and also reveal the size and structure of inner Earth.

OCEANIC CRUST
UPPER MANTLE
LOWER MANTLE
CONTINENTAL CRUST
OUTER CORE
INNER CORE

INNER INNER CORE

Recent findings show that the inner core has two layers: an outer inner core and an inner inner core. The magnetic poles of these two layers point in different directions. Just as the atom was peeled back to reveal protons, neutrons and electrons, which were then peeled back to reveal quarks, could scientists of the future discover an inner inner inner core and an outer inner inner core?

OUTER EARTH

The deepest human-made hole took about 20 years to dig, yet barely reaches 0.2% of the way to the centre of the Earth. This shows just how little we know about even the outermost layers of our planet...

PLATE TECTONICS

As early as 1596, people realised that Africa and South America looked like jigsaw pieces – could they have been joined in the past? It took several centuries for the idea of plate tectonics (slow-moving plates of crust which shift around the Earth's surface above the liquid mantle below) to be widely accepted. Geologists assembled the evidence and discovered that long ago there was one giant supercontinent, which they called Pangaea.

PANGAEA

ZEALANDIA

We already know that satellites helped to find thousands of undersea mountains. They've also discovered what several scientists believe to be a whole continent! Satellite data clearly shows a large area of continental crust rather than oceanic crust, though most of it is underwater. The islands of New Zealand and New Caledonia are some of the few spots above the surface. Time will tell how the world at large classifies this new discovery.

7.2 DEGREES

SIZE OF EARTH

Eratosthenes (276 BCE) lived in Alexandria. He used a stick to cast a shadow in the midday sun and calculated its angle to be 7.2 degrees (around one fiftieth of a circle). He knew that in another city, Syene, the Sun shone directly down a well at midday, casting no shadow. He realised that if he knew the distance between the two cities, he could calculate the world's circumference, which he did with amazing accuracy. His estimate was between 24,000km and 29,000 miles: we now know that the world's circumference is 40,073km (24,900 miles) at the equator.

4.4-BILLION-YEAR-OLD ROCK

In 2014, scientists announced they'd found zircon minerals in Australia that were about 4.4 billion years old – by far the oldest Earth rocks ever found (some meteors may be older). These hardy minerals were created shortly after the formation of the Earth. They have resisted pressure and temperature changes and have survived without being buried by layers of sediment. Their chemical composition shows us that the early Earth was a friendlier place for life to develop than we had previously thought.

NEW SPECIES... AND OLD ONES

Extinction is thought to happen at a natural or background rate of about one to five species per year. Scientists estimate we're currently losing species at a rate between 1,000 and 10,000 times the background rate. However, despite this sad statistic, scientists are continuing to discover new species at an astonishing rate.

SCIAPHILA SUGIMOTOI

Sciaphila sugimotoi is a rare type of plant. It doesn't get its energy from photosynthesis, instead feeding on other organisms. That's why it doesn't need green leaves, and its purple appearance gives it a somewhat alien look. It's only found on one small Japanese island.

LESULA MONKEY

The lesula monkey highlights the difference between formal scientific discovery and local discovery – the scientist that described the monkey found it living in someone's house! Clearly the monkey species had already been discovered before scientists came along and gave it a Latin name, Cercopithecus lomamiensis.

PSYCHEDELIC FROGFISH

The psychedelic frogfish (or Histiophryne psychedelica as it is officially known) is a remarkable-looking creature. Formally described by scientists in 2009, every individual has a unique pattern. They usually walk along the sea floor but can also turn themselves into a ball and use jet propulsion to move from place to place.

26

TAPANULI ORANGUTAN

These orangutans were well known to the locals of Sumatra, so why are they considered a new discovery? Well, scientists recently discovered that the orangutans of Batang Toru are genetically distinct from the Sumatran and Bornean orangutans, meaning that this isolated population of about 800 individuals is a new species, and a critically endangered one.

ATLANTIC FOREST TREE

This towering tree is tucked away in the dense Amazon Rainforest, which is why it has only been formally discovered in the last few years by scientists. It's probable though that local tribespeople have known about this species for centuries or even millennia.

OLD SPECIES... REDISCOVERED

Occasionally people have discovered live specimens of species which were thought to be extinct. This has happened with insects, birds, fish, dogs, trees, mushrooms, and even elephants. The two rediscovered species below are just the tip of the iceberg.

COELACANTH

This huge fish was thought to have gone extinct 66 million years ago. But in 1938, fisherman Hendrik Goosen caught one off the coast of South Africa, and museum curator Marjorie Courtenay-Latimer realised what it was.

AUSTRALIAN NIGHT PARROT

This bird was seen alive in 1912, then considered extinct after years of no sightings until – BAM – a car killed one in 1990 on a remote road. The death inspired photographer John Young to look for live specimens – and he was rewarded in 2013 after more than 17,000 hours of searching.

HIDDEN GEMS

Every once in a while, someone discovers a hidden gem in the Earth – either a literal one, such as gold, or a metaphorical one, like a wondrous cave. It makes us wonder what the next discovery will be, and who will be the discoverer.

GOLD

In 1848, James Marshall was building a sawmill beside a river in California. One morning, he got up to inspect the previous day's work and noticed something shiny in the water.

"BOYS, I BELIEVE I HAVE FOUND A GOLD MINE!"

Workers tried to break the metal with hammers to see if it really was gold and were sure that it was. Word quickly spread, and so the California Gold Rush began. Around 300,000 people came to seek their fortune… but only a lucky few ever struck gold.

A BIG HOLE

In 1991, Vietnamese logger Hồ Khanh got caught in a rainstorm. He was looking for a good spot to shelter in the forest when he came across the largest cave system (by volume) ever discovered! It has since been named Hang Son Doong, meaning 'cave of the mountain river'. After the find, Hồ Khanh gave up logging and became a conservationist and cave guide.

DEEP DISCOVERIES

Scientists were amazed that seismic waves showed the echoes of over a quadrillion tonnes of diamonds buried deep inside the planet. The diamonds are so deep – about 160km (99mi) below the surface – that humans will probably never be able to access them.

Even deeper, at 600km (373mi) or so, is another layer of diamonds. Known as ringwoodite, these minerals absorb water like a sponge, and it's been estimated that the ringwoodite layer contains more water than all the world's oceans put together. Astonishingly, John McNeill found a sample of this mineral on the surface in 2009.

Ringwoodite had previously only been found in meteorites, never on Earth. McNeill confirmed that it held water as suspected, and this discovery has changed our understanding of the structure of the Earth and the amount of water it holds.

28

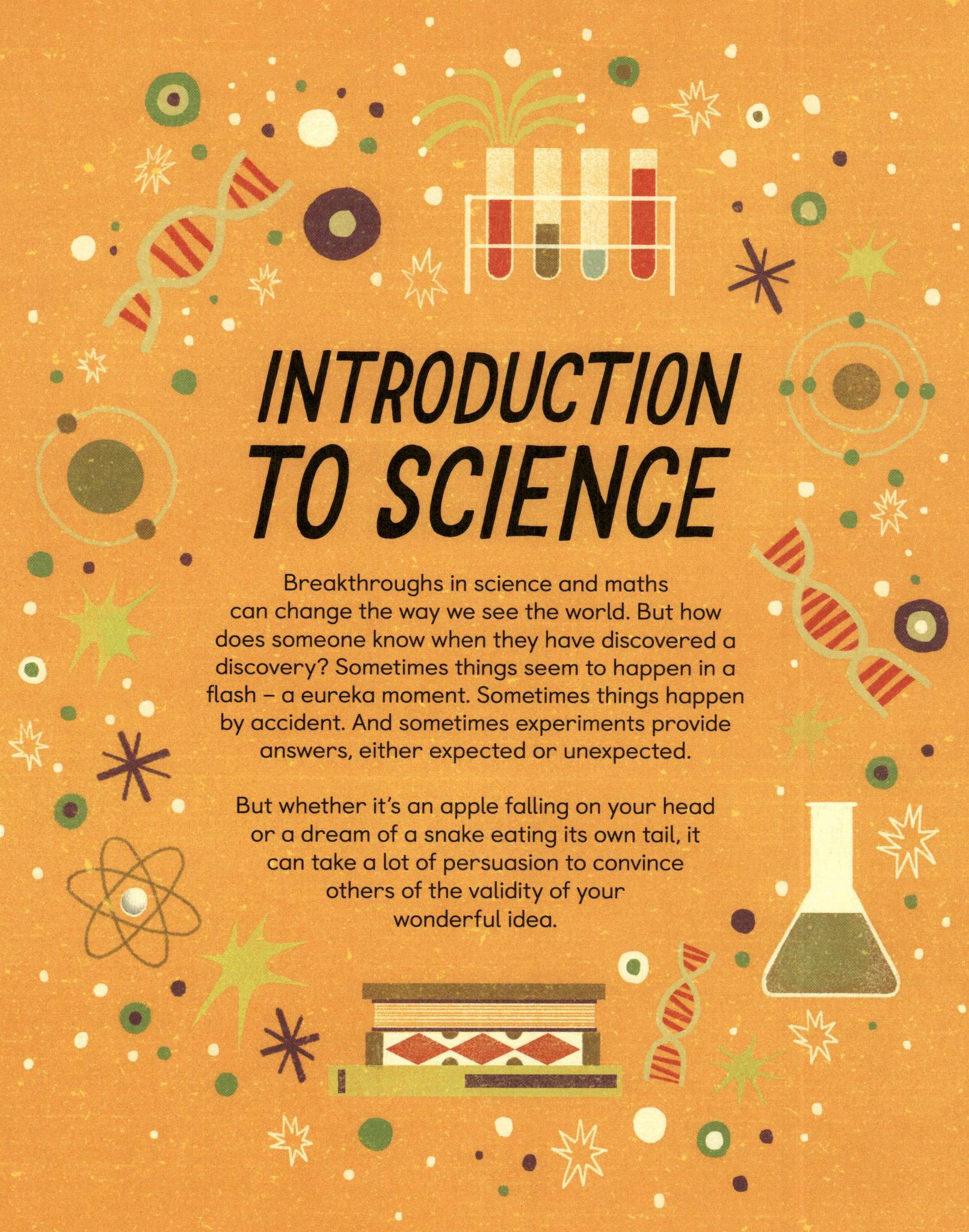

INTRODUCTION TO SCIENCE

Breakthroughs in science and maths can change the way we see the world. But how does someone know when they have discovered a discovery? Sometimes things seem to happen in a flash – a eureka moment. Sometimes things happen by accident. And sometimes experiments provide answers, either expected or unexpected.

But whether it's an apple falling on your head or a dream of a snake eating its own tail, it can take a lot of persuasion to convince others of the validity of your wonderful idea.

EUREKA MOMENTS

Sometimes discoveries are made in an *"AHA"* moment! Maybe you've experienced such breakthroughs yourself when doing something unrelated to solving the problem at hand – walking, sitting, or even sleeping. The subconscious brain may find new ways to tackle a problem while the conscious brain takes a break.

THE APPLE DROPPED

Legend has it that Isaac Newton discovered gravity when an apple fell on his head as he sat beneath an apple tree. But what's the core truth?

Newton's brainwave was more about the Moon than the apple – he realised it was constantly falling towards Earth but never reaching it, leading him to discover not just gravity but also laws of motion.

As for the apple – Newton's notebook does mention an apple tree in his Lincolnshire garden, but not an apple hitting his head. It makes for a juicy story though!

ARCHIMEDES

In 265 BCE Archimedes was asked by King Hiero II to find out whether his crown was pure gold or whether he'd been cheated.

But did he really make the discovery that heavier objects displace more water in his bathtub, then run naked through the streets shouting *"EUREKA!"* ("I've found it!")?

He certainly did make the discovery itself, but the story of running through the streets was first written 800 years later, so it is very unlikely to be true.

ARCHIMEDES

ISAAC NEWTON

30

IT'S ALL RELATIVE

One evening, Einstein heard the sounds of Bern's Zytglogge (time bell) and had a brainwave about the nature of time. As he imagined himself in a streetcar, travelling away from the clock at the speed of light, he realised that time ticks differently for different observers – this is a cornerstone of his theories of relativity.

Some accounts actually put Einstein in a streetcar on that evening, but that's just a fantasy element, as in the stories of Archimedes and Newton.

A WALK IN THE PARK

There's something about walking that clears the mind. History is littered with tales of walking epiphanies, including that of Nikola Tesla, who discovered how to use alternating current (which most electrical appliances rely on) and excitedly drew a diagram in the dirt with his walking stick.

William Hamilton, meanwhile, discovered how to multiply complex numbers (which have 'real' and 'imaginary' parts!) whilst walking by a canal and was so excited that he graffitied his idea onto the nearest bridge!

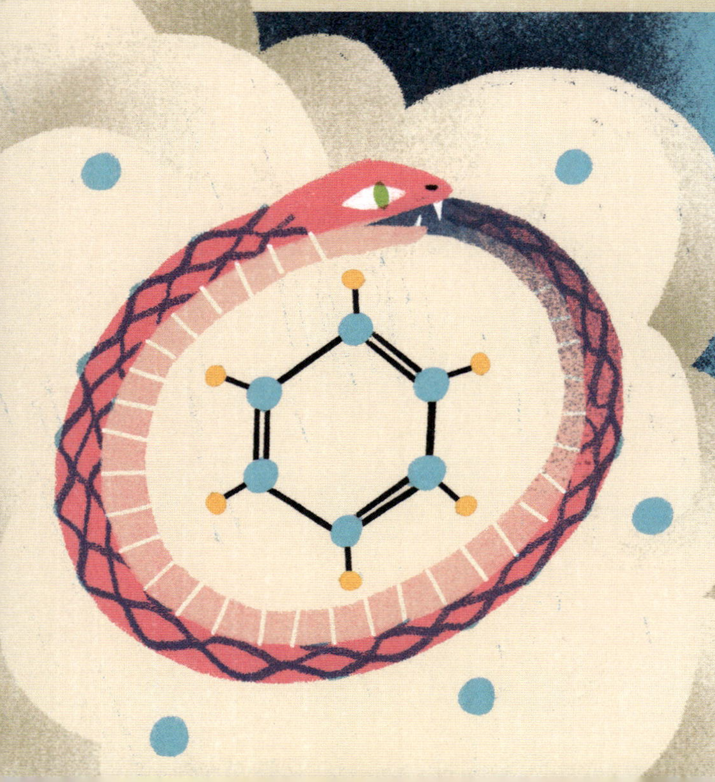

DREAMERS AND DAYDREAMERS

August Kekulé was struggling to work out the structure of benzene molecules when he dreamed of a snake eating its own tail one night. This revealed the answer to his puzzle as benzene molecules form complete rings.

Otto Loewi was studying nerve impulses, which he suspected were chemical rather than electrical, when he dreamt of a frog-based experiment. At first, the details were vague, but it came to him again the next night, and he performed the experiment as soon as he woke up!

ACCIDENTAL DISCOVERIES

Some discoveries are made entirely by accident. There's a famous example of a literal accident – a bar through a man's brain – which gave new insight as to how the brain works. Other discoveries are accidental in the unintentional sense rather than happening with a crash-bang-wallop. These ranged from a man who had a revelation whilst looking at a pile of washing-up to a pair of people who observed the echoes of the Big Bang without knowing it at the time.

A HOLE IN THE HEAD

"HERE IS BUSINESS FOR YOU!"

said railway worker Phineas Gage to his doctor after an accident caused an iron bar to pass through his head, taking out a chunk of his brain en route. After the accident Gage's personality was drastically different – overnight he became lazy and argumentative, and the railway had to fire him because of his behaviour.

Scientists realised that the brain affects personality and used Gage's accident to their advantage so that they could develop their theories more fully.

X-RAYS

Another medical breakthrough happened somewhat by accident. Wilhelm Roentgen was exploring electrical rays when he realised that in a dark room some mysterious rays were travelling through some objects while bouncing off others. He investigated with his own hand and saw straight through the flesh to his bones! His wife became his next experimental subject, and her wedding ring was observed as well as her bones.

FROG LEGS

Luigi Galvani was an 18th century Italian physiologist. He became convinced that electricity was linked to movement when his lab assistant was using a scalpel on the nerve of a dead frog's leg and he saw that a spark from a generator made the leg move. He set up an experiment outside, using a dead frog and a lightning rod, and waited for a thunderstorm. When the lightning flashed, energy coursed through the rod and made the frog's legs twitch!

PENICILLIN

Alexander Fleming had a collection of petri dishes from his experiments that he didn't wash up before he went on holiday. On his return, he was shocked to find a dish with no bacteria in a central area and realised he'd discovered the antibacterial agent penicillin – a 'miracle cure' had been found in a miraculous manner!

— PENICILLIUM COLONY
— STAPHYLOCOCCI (BACTERIA)
— STAPHYLOCOCCAL COLONY

PIGEON POO?

When Robert Wilson and Arno Penzias detected small levels of radiation coming from all directions into their radio telescope, they thought it must be a mistake – how could something be coming from everywhere? They concluded that their antenna had probably been contaminated with pigeon poo. After cleaning their equipment and continuing to detect radiation, they realised it was real. They had picked up the faint echoes of the Big Bang – a finding that changed human understanding of the entire universe.

EXPERIMENTAL DISCOVERIES

Whereas accidental discoveries came about by chance, experimental discoveries were arrived at by design. Sometimes the experimental apparatus would be incredibly simple – something you could do at home – but in other cases it would be colossally complicated, colossally expensive, and colossally COLOSSAL!

LOUIS PASTEUR

In 1859, Louis Pasteur boiled some broth in two flasks, one with a straight neck and the other with a curved neck. Several weeks later, the broth in the straight-necked jar had changed colour, but the broth in the curved-necked jar had not. This simple, elegant experiment showed that bacteria had passed through the straight neck and proved the germ theory of disease.

NEWTON'S PRISM

Newton performed a simple yet brilliant experiment to show that white light contains a spectrum of colours. He passed light through a glass prism, which separated the colours for all to see.

FRANKLIN'S KITE

Legend has it that Benjamin Franklin flew a kite in a thunderstorm experiment in 1752 and collected the charge in a jar to prove lightning's electrical nature.

FALLING BODIES

Many people claim that Galileo Galilei discovered that light and heavy objects fall at the same rate by dropping objects from the Leaning Tower of Pisa in 1589. There are two problems with this story:

(1) there is no evidence that Galileo performed such an experiment, and
(2) Simon Stevin had already made this discovery three years earlier by dropping balls from a tower in Delft.

STOPPING LIGHT IN ITS TRACKS

Light usually travels very fast but slows down when passing through materials such as glass or water. In 2001, Lene Vestergaard Hau from Denmark shocked the world when she was able to stop light altogether using ultra-cold atoms.

Despite reportedly wearing a silk shirt for safety, this is one of the more dangerous experimental set-ups that science has seen and is a triumph for daredevils!

PHOTOSYNTHESIS

In the 1600s, Jan Baptista van Helmont planted a willow tree in a pot. Over five years he took measurements and saw it gain mass (weight). This would have needed energy, which must have come from water and sunlight. This paved the way for an understanding of photosynthesis.

35

ELEMENTS

Ancient civilisations around the world used metals such as iron and tin, which we now know to be elements: matter all made from the same type of atoms.

There was a flurry of scientific discovery of elements in the 1700s and 1800s. Many were found experimentally, sometimes explosively. One was seen in the Sun rather than on Earth. And some were found to give out deadly radiation... which made discovery a dangerous business...

HELIUM

During a solar eclipse in 1868, multiple astronomers observed a strange spectral line coming from the Sun. It didn't match the signal of any known element, so they concluded it must be a new element, and named it after Helios, the Greek god of the Sun.

Cecilia Payne-Gaposchkin later discovered that hydrogen and helium are the most common elements in stars, and also the known universe.

PHOSPHORUS

German alchemist Hennig Brand tested any materials he could think of in his quest to make gold. In 1669 he boiled some urine, then heated the residue and noticed a flaming liquid. He'd discovered phosphorus from the most unlikely of ingredients!

OXYGEN

Who discovered oxygen? Well, Michael Sendivogius realised that air contained several gases, one of which was 'the food of life'. Carl Wilhelm Scheele first isolated the gas (which he called 'fire air'). Joseph Priestley experimented with mice and mint and was the first to publish his findings of 'dephlogisticated' life-giving air. And Antoine Lavoisier saw the nonsense of the 'phlogiston' theory and gave the gas the name oxygen.

THE PERIODIC TABLE

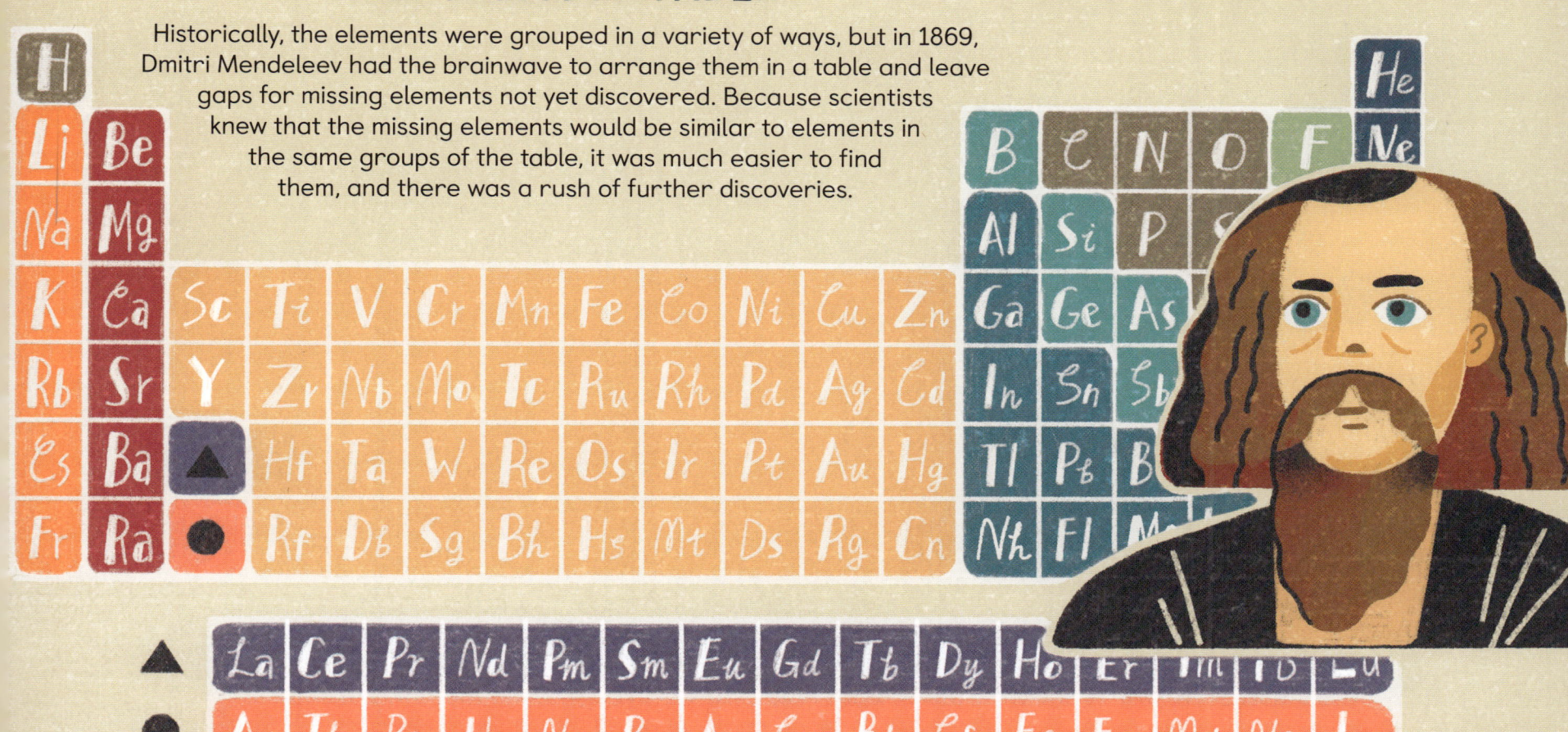

Historically, the elements were grouped in a variety of ways, but in 1869, Dmitri Mendeleev had the brainwave to arrange them in a table and leave gaps for missing elements not yet discovered. Because scientists knew that the missing elements would be similar to elements in the same groups of the table, it was much easier to find them, and there was a rush of further discoveries.

POLONIUM AND RADIUM

Marie Curie was a remarkable *DISCOVERER* – she won Nobel Prizes in physics and chemistry for her work on radioactivity and her discovery of two elements. She and her husband Pierre discovered the radioactive elements polonium and radium. Radioactive elements emit radiation and can be dangerous, but they can also be used to cure cancer and skin ulcers.

FRANCIUM

A student of Marie Curie called Marguerite Perey gained expert knowledge of the element actinium. When American scientists claimed to have found a new type of radiation coming from actinium in 1939, she couldn't believe it. She ran some tests and found that the radiation actually came from a new element. This element, francium, was the last element discovered in nature rather than made in a lab. Francium is so rare in nature that probably less than 30g (1oz) exists on Earth at any one time.

ATOMS

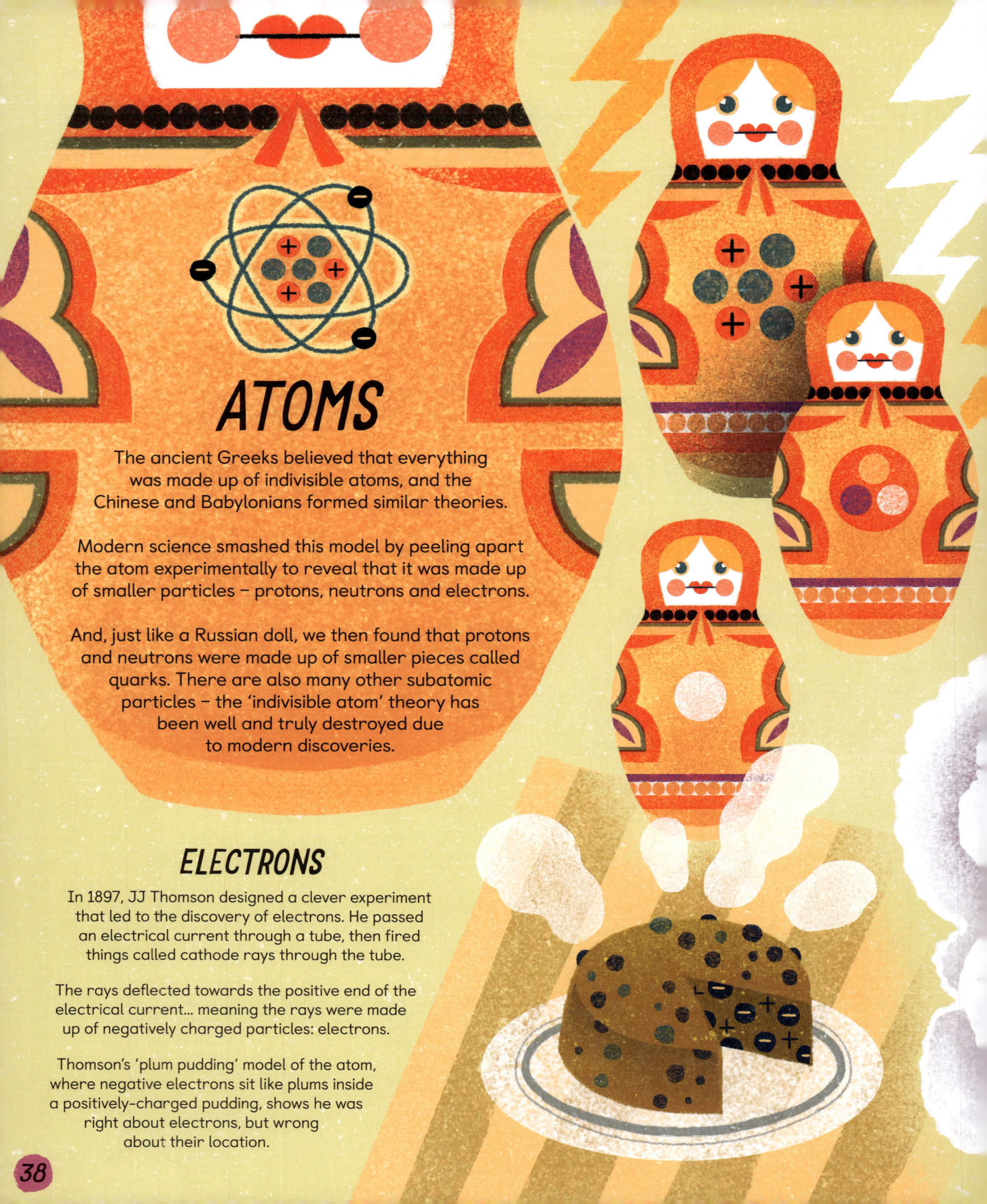

The ancient Greeks believed that everything was made up of indivisible atoms, and the Chinese and Babylonians formed similar theories.

Modern science smashed this model by peeling apart the atom experimentally to reveal that it was made up of smaller particles – protons, neutrons and electrons.

And, just like a Russian doll, we then found that protons and neutrons were made up of smaller pieces called quarks. There are also many other subatomic particles – the 'indivisible atom' theory has been well and truly destroyed due to modern discoveries.

ELECTRONS

In 1897, JJ Thomson designed a clever experiment that led to the discovery of electrons. He passed an electrical current through a tube, then fired things called cathode rays through the tube.

The rays deflected towards the positive end of the electrical current... meaning the rays were made up of negatively charged particles: electrons.

Thomson's 'plum pudding' model of the atom, where negative electrons sit like plums inside a positively-charged pudding, shows he was right about electrons, but wrong about their location.

PROTONS AND THE ATOMIC NUCLEUS

Ernest Rutherford is generally credited with the discovery of positively charged protons and the atomic nucleus. And he did design the experiment, but it was actually conducted by two of his assistants – Hans Geiger and Ernest Marsden. They fired positively charged alpha particles through gold foil. Most alpha particles passed straight through the gold, but a handful seemed to bounce back.

"IT WAS QUITE THE MOST INCREDIBLE EVENT THAT HAS EVER HAPPENED TO ME IN MY LIFE. IT WAS ALMOST AS INCREDIBLE AS IF YOU FIRED A 15-INCH SHELL AT A PIECE OF TISSUE PAPER AND IT CAME BACK AND HIT YOU."

ERNEST RUTHERFORD

Rutherford realised that there must be tiny areas of positive charge at the centre of the gold atoms... and so the atomic nucleus and the positively charged protons it contained were discovered.

NEUTRONS

The electron and proton were both discovered due to the effects of their electrical charges. But the neutral neutron was much more difficult to detect. Scientists began to see that atoms were heavier than expected – could there be something else in addition to protons and electrons?

In 1932, James Chadwick set up an experiment using a radioactive metal and some paraffin wax, and he thought he found evidence of neutral particles. He published a paper called 'Possible Existence of a Neutron'. Later, armed with new data, he was confident enough to publish 'The Existence of a Neutron'.

QUARKS

Protons, neutrons and electrons are not the end of the particle story. In ultra-high-energy laboratories, physicists smashed subatomic particles together and discovered that protons and neutrons are made up of smaller particles called quarks.

In 2017, Marek Karliner and Jonathan Rosner realised that certain quarks could fuse together, creating a huge explosion. They considered keeping their discovery secret so that it couldn't be used for bombs but then realised that although the explosion was powerful, it wouldn't set off a chain reaction like an atomic bomb.

BODIES AND BRAINS

Humans have put themselves under the microscope over the centuries and asked searching questions such as 'what makes us us?', 'how do our brains work?', and 'what's inside us?' Our self-knowledge is remarkably limited, but some surprising discoveries may change the way you look at yourself.

NEWFOUND HUMAN BODY PARTS

You'd have thought that all our body organs had been discovered long ago, but in the last few years scientists announced the discovery of the interstitium, an entirely new body part! This followed the rediscovery of the mesentery – a body part which had been known about for centuries, but which, on closer inspection, became classified by some as a 'new' organ.

CIRCULATION

A Greek physician called Galen discovered how the heart pumped blood around the body by observing dying soldiers and experimenting on animals. Several centuries later, Englishman William Harvey measured the volume of blood pumped around the body and concluded that the body didn't consume blood (as had been previously thought) – it went in a circuit from heart to body and back again.

THE DOUBLE HELIX

Biologists James Watson and Francis Crick discovered the structure of DNA, following Rosalind Franklin's study of DNA X-rays. In 1953 they observed DNA to be presented in a twisted-ladder shape called a double helix. This opened the floodgates for more discoveries in genetics – now individual genes can be isolated, 'read', and copied... so that cloning is now possible.

BRAINY BEHAVIOUR

Karl Spencer Lashley wanted to identify how and where memories were stored. He trained some rats to run through mazes, then he removed different percentages of their brains. (Yep, scientists can't be squeamish!)

He found that there was a gradual, but consistent, decline in the ability of the rats to remember the twists and turns of the maze. Lashley concluded that there is no single site for memory in the brain; it's stored across many pathways, and the brain can adapt.

DO WHAT I SAY!

In 1963, Stanley Milgram used members of the public for an experiment. Participants believed they were giving electric shocks to a 'learner', and were asked by an authority figure to increase the levels of electric shocks.

The shocks were fake and the 'learners' were actors, but Milgram saw that people tended to obey the authority figure, even if the level of electric shock was high enough to kill a human (if it had been real) – a truly shocking discovery!

ALL CREATURES GREAT AND SMALL

The Chukchi people of the Russian Far East have an encyclopaedic knowledge of reindeer, the Maasai know almost everything there is to know about lions, and the Warlpiri are experts on wallabies. Such discoveries have taken place across centuries of harmonious coexistence. 'Modern science' may be far behind, but it too has contributed to our understanding of the animal world via some remarkable discoveries.

MIGRATION MYSTERIES SOLVED

Swallows appear in Europe in the spring and disappear in the autumn, so Europeans wondered what happened to them the rest of the time. Some thought they transformed into robins (!) and a minister declared that they migrated to the Moon in the off-season (!!). It wasn't until relatively recently that their migration paths were tracked to Africa.

WOMAN AND BEAST

Jane Goodall studied chimpanzees for over 45 years. In 1960, in Tanzania, she observed a male called David Greybeard as he poked a stem of grass into a termite mound to 'fish' for termites, which would bite the grass stem and thus become David's snack.

We now know that our tool-wielding relatives include not just chimpanzees, orangutans and gorillas, but also octopuses, otters and crows.

JANE GOODALL

EVOLUTIONARY IDEAS

Darwin is credited for the theory of evolution but he wasn't the first to have such thoughts. The Chinese philosopher Zhuangzi (famous for dreaming of a butterfly and wondering if actually the butterfly was dreaming of him) wrote that animals were not in a fixed state but changed over time.

Darwin's own ideas didn't happen in the 'aha' moment many people imagine. His famous sketches showing the evolution of birds' beaks in the Galápagos were drawn years after he visited the islands and his observations of giant tortoises were somewhat incomplete… because he and his crew ate them all aboard their boat, the Beagle!

CHARLES DARWIN

ZHUANGZI

SEEING THE UNSEEN

In the seventeenth century, Dutch cloth merchant Antonie van Leeuwenhoek first developed powerful microscope lenses to study the quality of his cloth. He went on to study other things under the lenses, such as bees and lice, eventually discovering what he called 'little animals' – bacteria.

ANTONIE VAN LEEUWENHOEK

BEYOND EVOLUTION

Modern scientists are able to replicate and alter nature. Ears have been grown on the backs of mice, sheep have been cloned, and transparent zebrafish have been engineered. These fish give scientists a window into a new world and they are using their research to fight cancer, among other things.

ELEPHANTS' OTHER 'EARS'

Elephants can communicate over many kilometres and that's only partly due to their huge ears. A recent discovery showed that they use their feet to 'hear'. If a group of elephants becomes scared and stomps off – causing vibrations in the ground – another group of elephants several kilometres away can detect the vibrations and beat a retreat too.

MATHS

Many people mistakenly believe that there's nothing more to be discovered in maths, but that couldn't be further from the truth. There are many, many unknowns, and new discoveries are being made all the time – some simple, some complex, some beautiful, and some mysterious. When added to discoveries made over previous millennia, these findings help create a wonderful tapestry of our mathematical knowledge to date.

MEASUREMENT

René Descartes was a polymath – a genius in maths, philosophy, and pretty much anything he turned his mind to. One of his greatest discoveries came whilst having a lie-in. He noticed a fly on the ceiling and realised that if he drew a grid, he could state its position precisely. Just like that, a system of coordinates was conceived. We use his discovery all the time – from paper maps and mobile phones to plane and rocket guidance systems.

NUMBERS

Counting is as easy as one, two, three, right? Or should that be one, two, many (as some tribes' numerical vocabulary goes)? Or 1, 10, 11 (in binary numbers, as used by computers)? The truth is that numbers are deceptively complex things.

Zero is thought to have been first used by Indian mathematicians. At the other end of the scale, people around the globe use their computers to search for super-large prime numbers (numbers which can only be divided by 1 and themselves), and in 2018, a computer in Florida owned by Patrick Laroche found a prime number with almost 25 million digits – a new world record.

STATISTICS

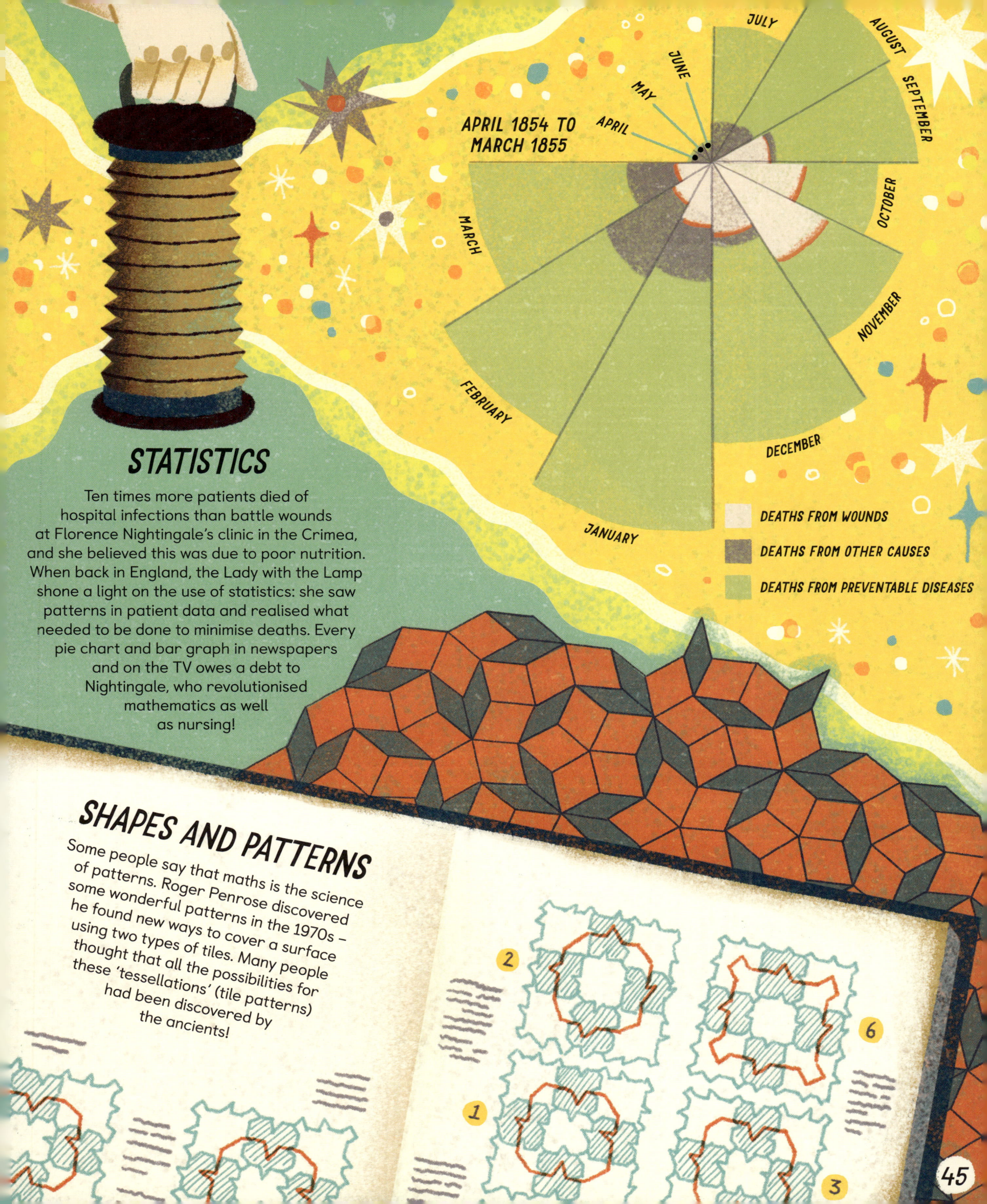

Ten times more patients died of hospital infections than battle wounds at Florence Nightingale's clinic in the Crimea, and she believed this was due to poor nutrition. When back in England, the Lady with the Lamp shone a light on the use of statistics: she saw patterns in patient data and realised what needed to be done to minimise deaths. Every pie chart and bar graph in newspapers and on the TV owes a debt to Nightingale, who revolutionised mathematics as well as nursing!

APRIL 1854 TO MARCH 1855

- DEATHS FROM WOUNDS
- DEATHS FROM OTHER CAUSES
- DEATHS FROM PREVENTABLE DISEASES

SHAPES AND PATTERNS

Some people say that maths is the science of patterns. Roger Penrose discovered some wonderful patterns in the 1970s – he found new ways to cover a surface using two types of tiles. Many people thought that all the possibilities for these 'tessellations' (tile patterns) had been discovered by the ancients!

45

BOTANICAL BREAKTHROUGHS

Humans discovered how to plant crops and grow food over 10,000 years ago, possibly in the Fertile Crescent in the Middle East. Around the world, wheat, barley and lentils were grown in the Middle East, sugarcane and bananas in New Guinea, potatoes in South America, rice in China, and maize in North America.

NEW SPECIES

Scientists are still discovering about 2,000 new species of plants every year. Some previously unknown plants include:

Kindia gangan, a member of the coffee family which scientists believe may help cure cancer.

Tahina spectabilis, a Madagascan palm which produces no flowers for 50 years or so, then puts so much effort into a spectacular bloom that it dies shortly afterwards.

Nepenthes biak, a carnivorous plant from New Guinea.

Oberholzeria etendekaensis, a hardy Namibian shrub, which was a rare double discovery as it was not only a new species but also a new genus (family of species).

TU YOUYOU

Born in China in 1930, Tu Youyou dreamed of helping others when she grew up. She studied traditional medicine and was placed on a secret government project to research treatments for malaria.

Tu Youyou experimented with thousands of plants and herbs and scoured ancient Chinese books about folk medicine. Finally she found what she was looking for: a plant called sweet wormwood. She fulfilled her wish of helping people, as drugs based on her discovery have saved millions of lives. She was awarded a Nobel Prize in Medicine in 2015.

GEORGE WASHINGTON CARVER

Born into slavery in around 1864, George Washington Carver became a famous botanist. He saw that cotton farmers produced better quality cotton if they planted sweet potatoes, soybeans, or peanuts in their cotton fields every few years to replace the nutrients in the soil.

Suddenly, American farmers had huge stocks of peanuts... and George Washington Carver solved this problem by developing hundreds of uses for peanuts, from Worcestershire sauce to cooking oil and from soaps to medicines.

INTRODUCTION TO SPACE

Space is a discoverer's dream. We've explored so little of it and have unravelled only a fraction of its many mysteries. Every time we send a rocket, shuttle, spaceship, or probe beyond our atmosphere, we come back with new knowledge. And every time we point a telescope towards the sky, discoveries are shining out at us, begging to be found.

Ancient civilisations were mesmerised by space, and they got a lot further then most modern astronomers could using their eyes and brains, rocks, sticks, and star charts. The telescope allowed people to see further and dream bigger.

AS OLD AS THE STARS

Humans living 1,000 years ago had far more practical knowledge about the positions of the stars than most people today. Signs in the sky were used for navigation, farming guidance, and to count time. It was obvious across cultures that a lunar month had about 28 days and a year had about 360 days, but many developed very accurate calendars using points such as the solstices (longest days or nights) and equinoxes (when there is an equal amount of day and night).

STONEHENGE

This stone circle in England is around 4-5,000 years old and is a perfect astronomical clock. Each year at the solstices, sunlight passes through the stone gate, and it used to shine on an altar stone. The level of precision to build this structure and to transport the stones over many miles is truly remarkable.

CHICHEN ITZA

In Mexico, there was a mighty city called Chichen Itza built by the Mayans over 1,000 years ago. Many of the structures still stand today, including a stone pyramid called El Castillo – The Castle. At the equinoxes, sunlight and shadow combine to look like a feathered snake sliding down the side of the pyramid – a spectacular sight.

POLYNESIAN NAVIGATION

Polynesians were masters of the seas, finding routes between tiny islands in an area of ocean greater than the size of Europe and Asia combined. They used various techniques and were highly skilled at reading the stars to tell them where they were heading. They passed down techniques of calculating angles and positions using their hands.

A NATURAL EGG TIMER

The Wiradjuri people of Australia keep a close watch of the position of the Great Celestial Emu, which the Western world knows as a part of the Milky Way. When the Emu is on the eastern horizon just after sunset, this means the emus are nesting, and there are no eggs to collect. But when the Emu's body is directly overhead after sunset, it's time for everyone to go and collect emu eggs.

WANDERING WORLDS

The Babylonians were the first to leave written records of Mercury, Venus, Mars, Jupiter, and Saturn. Whereas stars followed fixed paths through the sky, the planets seemed to wander. The ancient Greeks even called these objects 'planētēs', meaning 'wanderers'. A man called Philolaus suggested that these wanderers might move around a 'central fire'. Aristarchus went a step further and suggested the Earth and all the wanderers were in motion around the Sun. This solved the problem of the wanderers very neatly... but the idea was largely rejected for about 1,900 years.

SPOTTING A SUPERNOVA

On 4th July 1054, a massive supernova (exploding star) became visible and was seen for around two more years as a super-bright object. There is little evidence of the event in European records, but the Chinese and Arabs clearly documented the new object. The detailed observations represented the height of human knowledge of the stars at that time.

THE SOLAR SYSTEM

The 'wandering worlds' that the ancients saw were not the full story. The number of planets in our solar system has grown and then shrunk with new discoveries. Near space has thrown up as many surprises as deep space, from comets and dwarf planets to asteroids.

A REVOLUTIONARY IDEA

Nicolaus Copernicus often gets the credit for discovering that the Earth orbits the Sun but, as we've seen, Philolaus, Aristarchus and others also proposed a model where the Earth wasn't the centre of the universe.

Whilst brilliant, all these ideas were models or theories. It took many more brilliant brains – Galileo, Kepler and Newton, to name but three – to prove the Copernican model experimentally.

The idea was so difficult to accept that Copernicus delayed publication until shortly before his death, and Galileo was placed under house arrest because a Sun-centred system was deemed 'dangerous' by the authorities!

PLANETS AND DWARF PLANETS

In 1801, Giuseppe Piazzi announced the discovery of a new planet: Ceres. It has since been reclassified as a dwarf planet. At the time of its discovery in 1846, Neptune was considered the 13th planet, but it soon became the 8th, as five 'planets' were reclassified.

THE HERSCHELS

In 1781, William Herschel saw a faint object in the sky moving in front of the background of stars. He thought it was a comet but later realised it was a planet (Uranus) – the first to be discovered since ancient times. He also discovered multiple moons.

His sister, Caroline, was also a prolific astronomer – much, much more than just an assistant to William. She discovered at least eight comets and a new nebula and wrote about her discoveries in *COMETS AND LETTERS*.

NEPTUNE

URANUS

SATURN

JUPITER

THE MOON

What did the Moon landings teach us? They gave us samples of rock and dust to analyse, allowed us to walk on alien terrain, and the goal of a lunar landing itself led to many new discoveries in rocketry and the practicalities of space flight.

OTHER MOONS

There are more than 200 known moons in the Solar System. Even some dwarf planets such as Makemake have moons. Dutchman Christiaan Huygens discovered a moon of Saturn in 1655, which he named Titan. Worried in case anyone tried to claim the discovery for themselves, he cleverly published the discovery in an anagram (jumbled letters) and only later revealed the meaning!

THE BLUE MARBLE

A 1972 photograph from the Apollo 17 spacecraft has allowed millions of us to discover a new view of our planet. It's one of the most viewed photos in human history.

COMETS

In 1705, Edmund Halley realised several historical comets with the same path were, in fact, the same object. He predicted its next arrival in 1758/9. Sadly, he wasn't around to see what is now known as *HALLEY'S COMET*.

3753 CRUITHNE

Only one true moon orbits Earth, but there are up to 18,000 Near Earth Objects, some of which have been claimed as second moons by excited discoverers. One such example is 3753 Cruithne, which orbits the Sun in a horseshoe pattern.

GALILEO GALILEI & SIMON MARIUS

Few people have made as many important discoveries as an Italian called Galileo Galilei. He discovered that heavy and light objects accelerate at the same rate (though others worked on this too), he improved the telescope, and he discovered craters on the Moon, spots on the Sun, rings around Saturn, and four moons orbiting Jupiter, which are now known as the Galilean moons. Many of his important findings were published in a book called Sidereus Nuncius, meaning *STARRY MESSENGER*.

A German known as Simon Marius was a great rival of Galileo. He too discovered the same four moons of Jupiter as Galileo and published his results in Mundus Jovialis, *THE WORLD OF JUPITER*. Both men claim they got there first. Centuries later, a jury considered their cases and concluded that the two men had independently discovered the moons at almost exactly the same time.

51

DEEP SPACE

Space is MIND-BOGGLINGLY big. In 2012, about 35 years after being launched, Voyager 1 became the first manmade object to leave the solar system, but it won't pass the next star for 40,000 years!

Our knowledge of space comes almost entirely from afar – what can our eyes and telescopes detect and how can we interpret data from millions of light years away?

GOING INTERGALACTIC

In 1925, American astronomer Edwin Hubble discovered that some distant light sources were way beyond the Milky Way. He recognised whole new galaxies and classified them according to their shape. Before this, people thought that the entire universe consisted of the Milky Way galaxy.

In 2003, scientists announced they'd discovered a new galaxy in our own backyard: the Canis Major Dwarf Galaxy. Not everyone agrees that it's a galaxy – some call it an 'overdensity of stars' – but no one expected to find such a structure of stars much closer than the Andromeda Galaxy, which we used to think of as our next-door neighbour.

PROTOPLANETARY DISC

PILLARS OF CREATION

FOMALHAUT SYSTEM

WINDOW TO THE WORLD

The Hubble Space Telescope has taken billions of photographs of galaxies, quasars, supernovae, and more, aiding millions of discoveries. Its super-powerful light detectors can probe further into the depths of space than ever before.

The Hubble Space Telescope will be replaced by the even more powerful James Webb Space Telescope, which is set to deliver millions of discoveries about our beautiful universe.

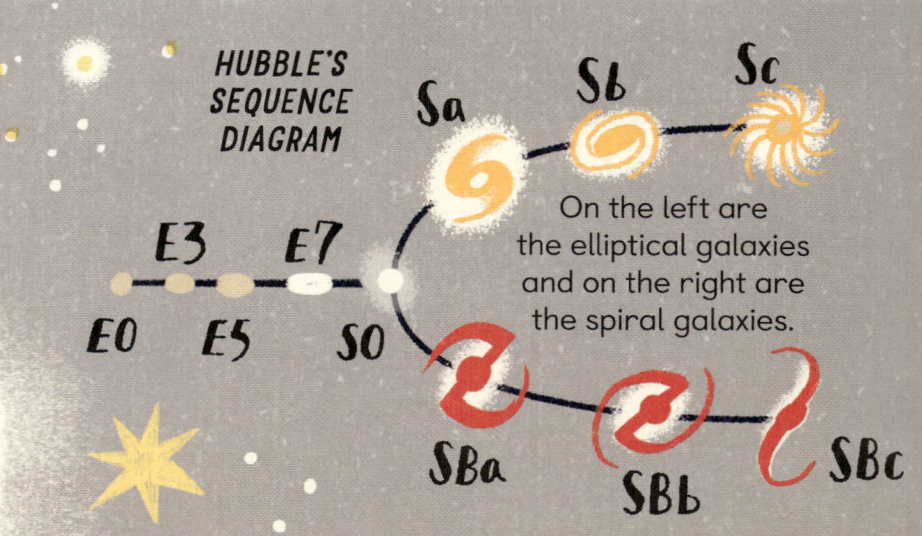

HUBBLE'S SEQUENCE DIAGRAM

Sa Sb Sc

E3 E7

E0 E5 S0

SBa SBb SBc

On the left are the elliptical galaxies and on the right are the spiral galaxies.

IS ANYBODY OUT THERE?

The search for extraterrestrial life focuses on finding exoplanets – planets outside our solar system. These are tricky to find because they are small and dark, unlike the big, bright stars they orbit. So far, about 4,000 have been discovered, a handful of which appear to be in the GOLDILOCKS ZONE – not too close and not too far from their sun, meaning there's a chance they could support life.

The earliest evidence of an exoplanet was recorded in 1917. Adriaan van Maanen discovered a star that became known as van Maanen 2. Walter Sydney Adams recorded the star's spectrum – its chemical fingerprint. Modern astronomers now recognise that the spectral pattern is evidence of exoplanets around the star.

Those faint lines might seem strange evidence for exoplanets, but it is almost impossible to spot faraway worlds because planets themselves do not emit light.

DARK SPACE

A lot of space is dark, but certainly not dull. Because we historically detected distant objects by their light, dark objects have always been shadier characters to capture – sometimes we can see their effects on light-emitting neighbours via gravity or movement or spectra. Exoplanets are a prime example. However, there's a lot more dark matter hiding out of sight than exoplanets...

"I WOULD PREFER TO STAY UP AND WATCH THE STARS THAN GO TO SLEEP".

VERA RUBIN

DARK MATTER

Vera Rubin observed galaxies in all directions of the sky through her telescope and realised something was odd. The spin of the galaxies couldn't be explained by conventional science... unless there were heaps of invisible matter providing a gravitational pull. Rubin had found the first evidence of mysterious dark matter, which scientists now believe makes up around 27% of all matter in the universe!

GRAVITATIONAL WAVES

Einstein's theory of relativity predicted gravitational waves back in the early twentieth century. A Nobel Prize was awarded in 1993 for indirect evidence of these waves in far star systems. But could anyone find direct evidence? It wasn't until 2015 that two ultra-sensitive sensors were tickled by a gravitational wave. Scientists were observing ripples caused by the ancient collision of two black holes, and another Nobel Prize was awarded for this discovery in 2018.

DARK ENERGY

When looking into deep space, astronomers also look back in time, as the light from distant sources has taken billions of years to reach their telescopes. They noticed that about 7.5 billion years ago, the rate of expansion of the universe accelerated sharply. Just as a car needs energy to accelerate, so too does a universe. Since scientists cannot see the source of the energy, they've labelled it as dark energy. Despite several theories, no one knows for sure what form it takes.

54

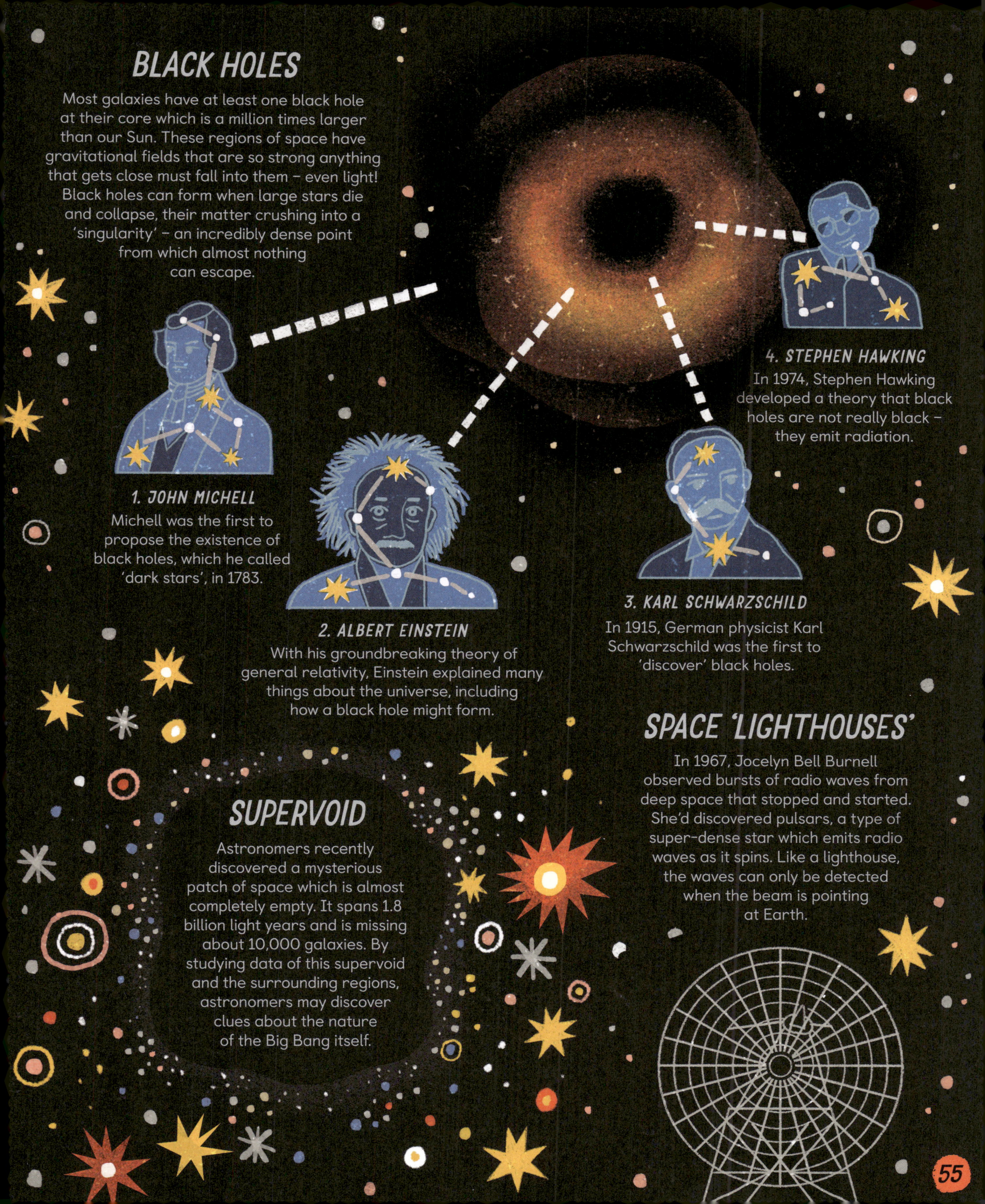

BLACK HOLES

Most galaxies have at least one black hole at their core which is a million times larger than our Sun. These regions of space have gravitational fields that are so strong anything that gets close must fall into them – even light! Black holes can form when large stars die and collapse, their matter crushing into a 'singularity' – an incredibly dense point from which almost nothing can escape.

1. JOHN MICHELL
Michell was the first to propose the existence of black holes, which he called 'dark stars', in 1783.

2. ALBERT EINSTEIN
With his groundbreaking theory of general relativity, Einstein explained many things about the universe, including how a black hole might form.

3. KARL SCHWARZSCHILD
In 1915, German physicist Karl Schwarzschild was the first to 'discover' black holes.

4. STEPHEN HAWKING
In 1974, Stephen Hawking developed a theory that black holes are not really black – they emit radiation.

SUPERVOID

Astronomers recently discovered a mysterious patch of space which is almost completely empty. It spans 1.8 billion light years and is missing about 10,000 galaxies. By studying data of this supervoid and the surrounding regions, astronomers may discover clues about the nature of the Big Bang itself.

SPACE 'LIGHTHOUSES'

In 1967, Jocelyn Bell Burnell observed bursts of radio waves from deep space that stopped and started. She'd discovered pulsars, a type of super-dense star which emits radio waves as it spins. Like a lighthouse, the waves can only be detected when the beam is pointing at Earth.

STRANGE SPACE

Hidden moons, other worlds, black holes, dark matter, dark energy, gravitational waves... that's all rather average in the weird world of space. Here are just a few truly **BAFFLING** discoveries...

TWINKLE, TWINKLE, LITTLE STAR, HOW WE WONDER WHAT YOU ARE. UP ABOVE THE WORLD SO HIGH, LIKE A DIAMOND IN THE SKY.

THE PLANET WITH A DIAMOND CORE

In the nursery rhyme, stars twinkle like diamonds, but stars aren't really made of diamonds, right? Well... PSR J1719-1438 b is an unusual star: it turned into a planet with a diamond core at the end of its life.

Stranger still, it orbits a neutron star called 1438 which is so dense that a teaspoon of it would weigh more than a billion tonnes on Earth, and 1438 spins at about 10,000 times a minute, sending out huge pulses of radio waves.

GIANT ALCOHOL CLOUD

A huge alcohol cloud, spanning 288 million light years, has been discovered deep in space. It naturally amplifies microwaves in a parallel process to the way lasers amplify visible light.

LASER means Light Amplification by Stimulated Emission of Radiation, and methyl alcohol clouds use MASER (Microwave Amplification by Stimulated Emission of Radiation); the same thing, but with a different wavelength. So when scientists thought they'd discovered LASER technology, they'd sort of been beaten to it by alcohol clouds in deepest, darkest space!

56

UNUSUAL ASTEROIDS

Comets have tails, but asteroids rarely have them. So it was a huge surprise when in 2013 an asteroid was discovered with six tails, belching out dust.

"WE WERE LITERALLY DUMBFOUNDED,"

David Jewitt of the University of California said in a statement from NASA. "Even more amazing, its tail structures change dramatically in just 13 days."

Earlier that year, a different team of astronomers had discovered an asteroid with rings orbiting the Sun between Saturn and Uranus. Previously, rings were only thought to form around planets classified as gas giants.

LOOKING AHEAD

Astronomers of the past worked on their own or in small teams. Today, international projects are the norm, and many discoveries are made not by looking at the sky but by looking at data. Today's most powerful telescopes produce so much data that it can take years to analyse. Tomorrow's telescope – the Square Kilometre Array – is expected to produce 700 terabytes of data a day, which will undoubtedly lead to millions of discoveries.

UNDISCOVERED SPACE

Much of space is undiscovered. In terms of physical exploration, we've barely left our front door and have only made a handful of journeys to our nearest neighbouring space rocks. Space is a huge entity inviting exploration and discovery. Some of this is done by satellites, shuttles, rovers, and space telescopes. But the amateur sitting at home can contribute too, using a home computer's power to sift through data from powerful space telescopes – people are finding new stars, galaxies, quasars, and more all the time.

But there are limits to what we can see and discover about space...

THE UNOBSERVABLE UNIVERSE

We cannot see most of the universe and will never be able to, unless wormholes or other faster-than-light methods are used. (These would be huge discoveries, but if time travel were possible, then why haven't people from the future been to visit us?)

This is because space and time are linked. When we see sunlight, it's come from 8 minutes and 20 seconds in the past. Although light travels super-fast at 300,000 km (186,411mi) per second, it has to travel a super-large distance – 150 million km (93 million mi).

58

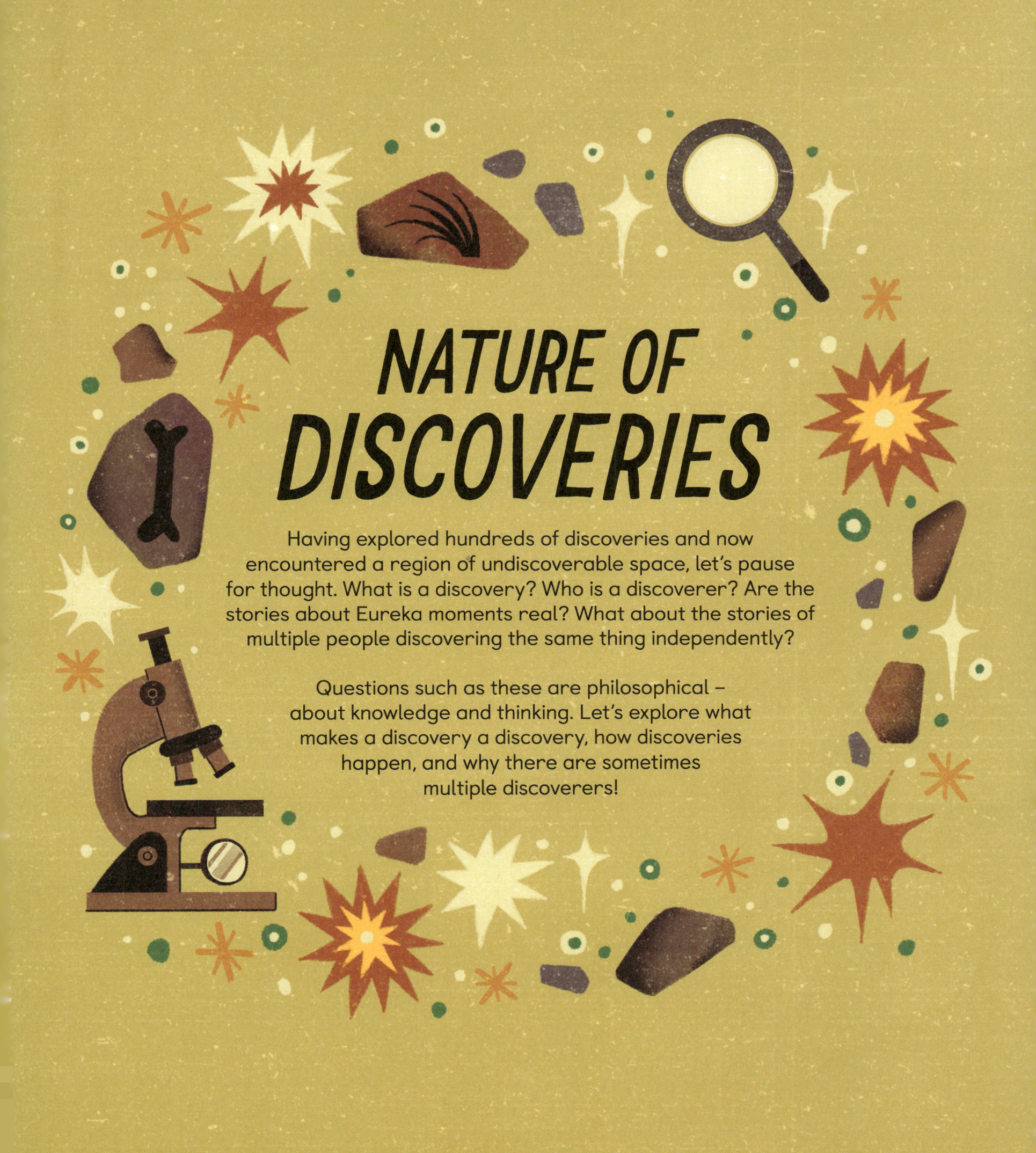

NATURE OF DISCOVERIES

Having explored hundreds of discoveries and now encountered a region of undiscoverable space, let's pause for thought. What is a discovery? Who is a discoverer? Are the stories about Eureka moments real? What about the stories of multiple people discovering the same thing independently?

Questions such as these are philosophical – about knowledge and thinking. Let's explore what makes a discovery a discovery, how discoveries happen, and why there are sometimes multiple discoverers!

AGAINST THE ODDS

Societies haven't always been equal. There have been times and places when about 50% of the population has been denied the vote, university degrees and professorships. There have been times when the other 50% of the population have taken sole credit for shared discoveries. Despite all of these obstacles, women have made countless remarkable discoveries, such as these...

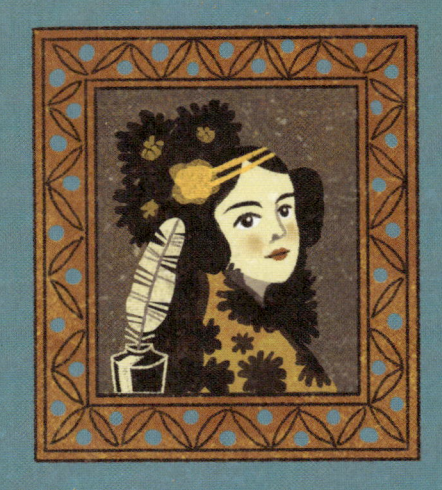

Born in 1815, Ada Lovelace was an English mathematician, often regarded as one of the first computer programmers.

10th century AD Mariam al-Asturlabiyy was an astronomer living in what is now northern Syria.

Born in Vienna in 1878, Lise Meitner led the way in discoveries about nuclear fission.

Maria Goeppert Mayer developed the nuclear shell model. She described the orbiting electrons as waltzers, spinning around the nucleus. Another team of scientists later arrived at the same idea independently, and they shared the Nobel Prize.

Born in 1647, Maria Merian was a German who made numerous discoveries about insects, especially their metamorphosis.

A woman known only as Fang is credited with "the discovery of how to turn mercury into silver" – possibly the chemical process of boiling off mercury in order to extract pure silver residue from ores.

In 1650 Maria Cunitz published an accurate method for predicting the paths of planets, massively improving upon the work of the much more famous Johannes Kepler.

Hildegard von Bingen was a medieval nun who wrote extensively about the use of plants, herbs and healing stones, and about physical symptoms and cures. She has since become a saint.

Jeanne Dumée was a 17th century astronomer who wrote a book supporting the theories of Copernicus. She firmly believed that women were as smart as men at subjects like maths and science!

Born in around 1200 BCE, Tapputi of Babylon is considered by many to be the world's first recorded chemist. She concocted perfumes and medicines for the king.

Mathematicians had always thought that a piece of paper, no matter what its size, could only be folded in half seven times. But in 2002, American high school student Britney Gallivan produced an equation, bought a special $85 1.2km (0.7mi) roll of toilet paper, then stunned the world by folding it in half twelve times.

In 1967, Jocelyn Bell Burnell discovered pulsars, a type of super-dense star which emits radio waves as it spins.

Katie Bouman paved the way for the first incredible image of a black hole and its super-bright surrounding disc of stars and other matter being pulled in. It was captured by the Event Horizon telescope in 2019.

Nancy Grace Roman is often known as 'the mother of Hubble', as she led the team who prepared the telescope.

American Katherine Johnson worked for NASA and became a 'human computer' who calculated flight paths for space missions… which had to be accurate to bring the astronauts back alive.

ANATOMY OF DISCOVERIES

Discoveries are moments when new knowledge is found. So if a man dug up a curiously shaped fossil and took it to a museum where a woman identified it as a tooth of a new dinosaur species, you could say the man discovered the fossil but the woman discovered the species. Or you could say that both contributed to the discovery of the species. Or you could argue, bitterly!

BUT I DISCOVERED WHAT IT WAS!

I DISCOVERED IT!

DISCOVERY OF DISCOVERIES

Sometimes we don't discover discoveries until years, decades, centuries, or millennia later. A good example is the discovery of Australia. As we've seen, a recent find of Aboriginal tools means that humans discovered Australia thousands of years earlier than we had previously thought. Through new evidence, we discovered an earlier discovery.

THAT'S A NEW SPECIES!

At other times we discover objects but don't quite realise what they are. The new knowledge part of the discovery can come years later. The Louisiana pancake batfish is a classic example – it was 'discovered' in a museum when someone realised it was a new species!

FALSE DISCOVERIES

Sometimes a discovery is declared, but it later turns out to be a false alarm. For example, sometimes a new species has been claimed which turned out to be a juvenile specimen of a previously known species. This happened with Brontosaurus... it was actually a juvenile specimen of Apatosaurus. Museums changed their labels and dinosaur books were rewritten.

But the latest twist is that some scientists have re-examined fossils and think that the Brontosaurus was a separate species after all... meaning there could have been a false 'false discovery'!

MULTIPLE DISCOVERIES

Sometimes several people make discoveries independently at about the same time. We've seen how Benjamin Franklin may have discovered electricity with a kite in a storm in 1749. But the story wouldn't be complete without a mention of Czech theologian Prokop Diviš, who tried to prevent thunderstorms from happening and who 'invented' the lightning rod in 1754, probably without knowledge of Franklin's work.

These multiple discoveries raise an interesting point: when does a discovery become a discovery? The moment of knowledge could occur any time, but historians often quote the date when the knowledge was published. So discoverers usually race to write down their findings to make sure they get credit.

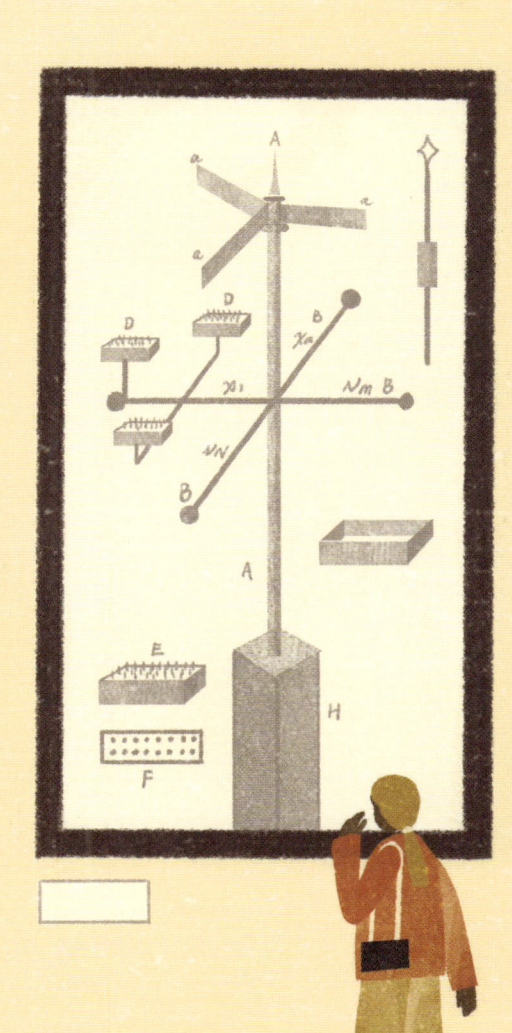

63

WHATEVER NEXT?

A world of discovery is all around us. New knowledge about things big and small, near and far, delicate and dangerous is being uncovered even as you are reading this sentence!

Biologists are recording new species in the rainforests and oceans, scientists are working on cures for cancer, mathematicians are in the midst of searches for super-large prime numbers, archaeologists are piecing together information about ancient civilisations, palaeontologists are digging up new dinosaurs, and astronomers are pointing their telescopes deep into space and searching for answers about life, the universe, and everything.

But discoveries are not made only by professionals. They can happen to anyone, anywhere at any time, and they favour those with open eyes and open minds. What discoveries will be made in your lifetime?